WELCOME TO
YOUTHSEARCH!

If you have limited time to prepare to lead your YOUTHSEARCH group, look at QUICKSCAN™ on page 3. You will find enough basic information in QUICKSCAN™ to help you get started.

YOUTHSEARCH offers you an opportunity to work closely with other people and to learn about topics that are crucial concerns of everyday life. YOUTHSEARCH is designed

✔ to help you prepare to lead a group;

✔ to give you plenty of practical ideas and options;

✔ to be faith-oriented and biblically based;

✔ to help you build rapport so that group members are willing to share honestly their concerns, questions, and insights;

✔ to be easy to use.

You may have decided to form a small group because you and people you know are concerned about a particular subject. We hope that by completing the sessions in this book, you will

✔ learn ways of inviting people into your group and of making them feel welcome;

✔ gain insight into yourself, your life, and the lives of the youth in your group;

✔ understand how the Bible and Christian faith apply to issues affecting you and the other members of your group;

✔ see other ways for people to work together in small groups.

We believe that YOUTHSEARCH will help youth and adults to struggle together with questions about how to live faithfully. As the members of the group begin to work together, they will

✔ offer one another support and encouragement as they grow in faith and become the people God wants them to be;

✔ listen to one another actively and effectively to become aware of what is most important in their lives.

The secret energy of YOUTHSEARCH is in your group. Every group is a unique combination of personalities and abilities. This book is simply a tool to guide and support the members of your group as they learn and grow together in faith.

Regardless of the order in which you use them, the books in the YOUTHSEARCH series build on one another. Each book will introduce skills that you can use in future small-group study.

If you are the leader of a Youth-Search group, please read the articles in the back of this book. They will answer some of your questions and will help you prepare to lead the group. If you are a participant, you may want to read the leader's articles in order to learn ways of helping the leader and of developing rapport among members of the group.

We want to share your excitement about using YOUTHSEARCH. We also want to hear about your concerns. If you have any questions about YOUTHSEARCH, feel free to call Curric-U-Phone at 1-800-251-8591 and to ask for the editor of YOUTHSEARCH.

Have a terrific time with your YouthSearch group!

Your editorial team for this volume of YOUTHSEARCH:

Diana L. Hynson
editor

John J. Rudin, III
assistant editor

Branson L. Thurston
coordinating editor

QUICKSCAN™

For an overview of each session, use QUICKSCAN.™

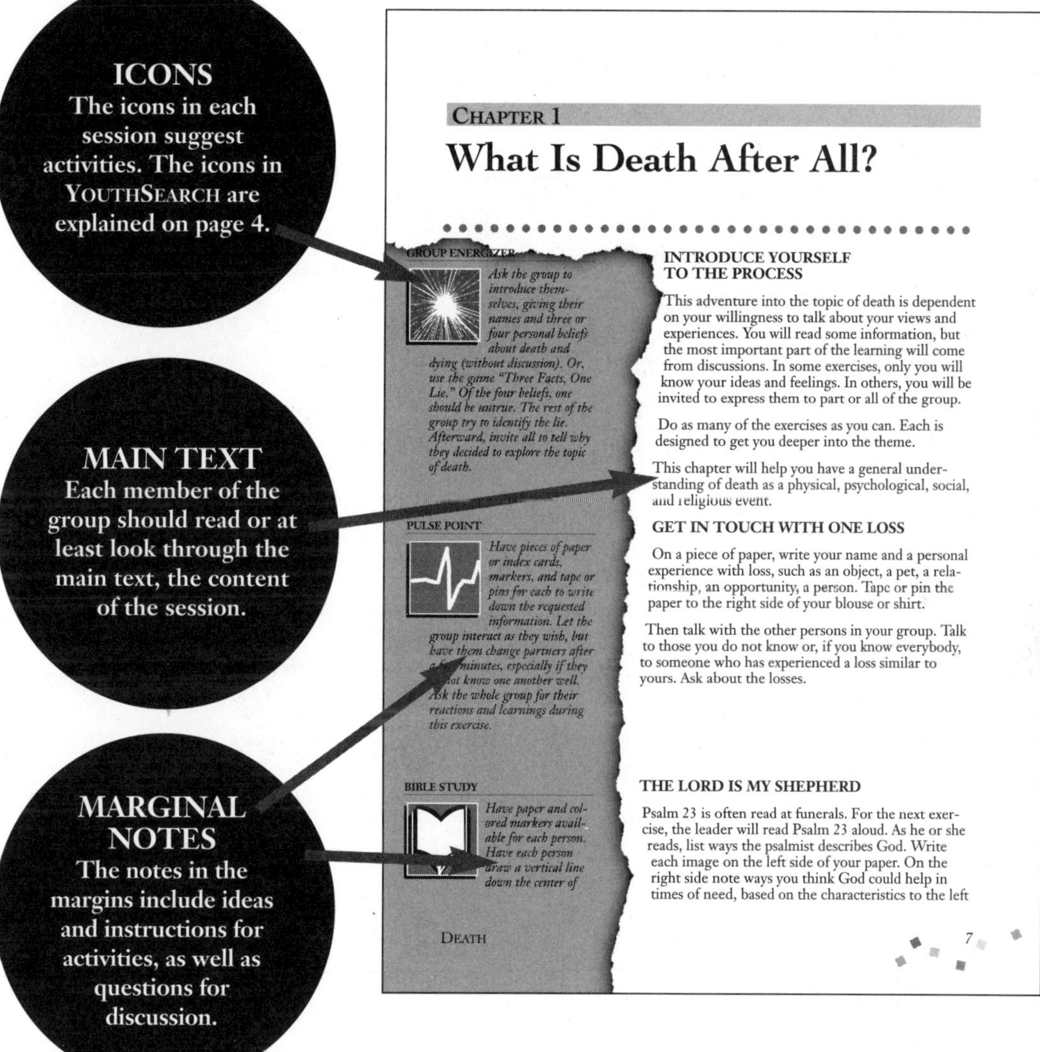

For more help preparing to lead a YouthSearch group, read "Welcome to YOUTHSEARCH!" beginning on page 1 and the articles in the back of the book.

ICONS

Icons are pictures or symbols that will show you, at a glance, what to do in each part of the session. These are the icons used in YOUTHSEARCH:

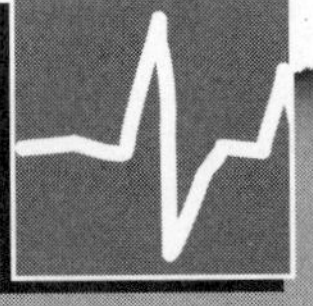

PULSE POINT indicates a time to assess the group's feelings and to find out what's been happening in the participants' lives since their last meeting.

GROUP ENERGIZER refers to an activity that focuses the group's attention on the topic. The energizer may be an ice-breaker at the beginning of the session or an activity during the session that gets the group excited about the topic.

WORSHIP means a time of prayer, music, guided meditation, or celebration.

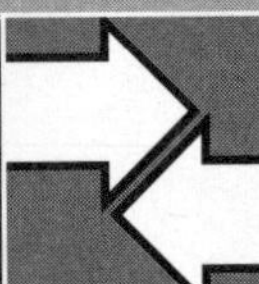

DISCUSSION asks you to engage members of the group in discussion by asking questions such as those listed in the marginal notes.

GROUP INTERACTION indicates an activity such as a role-play, simulation, or small group discussion that involves members of the group in learning together.

BIBLE STUDY asks you to invite the group to explore a Bible passage.

REFLECTION indicates a time of quiet reflection on an issue or a question.

DECISION POINT alerts you to consider a decision about 1) including new members in the life of the group, 2) dividing the chapters so that they can be used for more than one period of time, 3) extending a chapter beyond one session because of the group's interests or concerns.

BEFORE NEXT TIME identifies what leaders and/or participants will need to prepare for the next session.

INTRODUCTION

eath evokes different reactions from us at different stages of our lives. The first time I heard about death it didn't have much meaning for me; I was only four. My grandfather died. My family had taken care of him at home for a long time. For me the only thing strange was that Grandpa spent all his time in bed and the rest of us were supposed to be good to him. So when I heard Grandma and Mother and my uncles crying, death meant distress.

Soon there was a lot of activity in the house as neighbors came to visit. I spent several hours with a neighbor who had a child my age and later learned about my grandpa's funeral. Grandma had difficulty keeping me quiet. At four? And with so many people around me? Having so many people around was an invitation to play. But Grandma told me that was not proper.

Death carried other meanings later in life. As other members of the family and some friends died, I discovered that my reactions were different. Death was not anything like playing; death had very somber tones.

Death hits you in different ways depending on your relationship with the person or persons who have died. Your reaction to death will be similar to your reaction to other losses in your life at that age. How you deal with death and grief is determined by what spiritual and psychological resources you can tap.

Thus my reactions to my sister's death when I was thirty-five or to my father's death when I was forty-one were different from my playful reaction to my grandpa's death when I was four. At forty-one, I found losses had special meanings. Crying made more sense than playing. But prayer and the support of family and friends were available. My life in the church had taught me important lessons about life, death, and hope that I could rely on in times of need.

Death: This Study

By the time your group have worked through this study I hope that you will have a better understanding of the Christian perspective of death and that you will be able to talk to others about death with confidence. I also hope that you too will have spiritual and psychological resources you can tap when death affects you personally.

This study resource has six chapters. Each chapter has regular sections. At the beginning of each chapter Pulse Point encourages you to talk about ideas and feelings you have had during the week. The first chapter invites you to keep a journal or diary. Journalling will make the discussion and reflections personal. Journalling also allows you to explore this topic with your feelings and will as well as your mind.

Each chapter also includes group energizers, worship, discussion, group interaction, Bible study, and decision-making about the life of the group. Some chapters include assignments for the next meeting time.

Chapter 1 is an overview of different issues related to death. You will discuss some physical, psychological, social, and religious descriptions and implications of death. Chapter 2 will explore different ways death occurs for persons. Even when death is considered the end of the lifelong process of aging, the actual causes of death are varied. But most youth who die do so as a result of violence, automobile accidents, or suicide.

Discussion of ways death can affect you personally when you lose someone you care about is included in Chapter 3. The discussions and exercises allow you to consider your feelings about people you might still remember. In Chapter 4 you will learn some skills that will help you support others going through hard times.

If you are unsure about how to act at a funeral or how to comfort a grieving person, Chapter 5 will be helpful. It also includes information and discussion questions about legal matters related to death. Chapter 6 offers an overview of basic Bible teachings on death.

The last chapter also asks you to consider your overall view of death after studying this resource. By then I expect you to view death differently than you now do. And I hope that you will be able to talk to others about death with confidence, as well as offer support and comfort to anyone affected by the death of another.

And What About You?

Why did you decide to join this group? Maybe something has happened in your life that you want to understand. This resource and interaction with other persons in your group will help you understand the meaning of life and death in the context of the Christian faith.

If you are in this group because someone close has died or is dying, I pray that you will be comforted as you go through this study. Such assistance might also include an overview of the professional help available to you. I hope that members of your group will become good friends, offering you and others support for difficult times in your lives.

You might want to know more about death just to be a better friend. I hope that this resource will help you cultivate the skills for hearing and responding to the needs of others in appropriate ways. For instance, you or some of your friends might be exposed to at-risk situations. Or you might live in a neighborhood with limited personal security. Or you may have felt uncomfortable at some time because you did not know how to respond to the needs of others. This resource should offer you practical advice for such situations.

Above all, I pray that you will be able to understand that death is part of being human and part of life, that grief is part of a process with the potential to help you grow, and that Jesus Christ is the foundation of our Christian hope when death affects our lives.

—Carmen M. Gaud

Carmen M. Gaud is an ordained member of the Methodist Autonomous Affiliated Church of Puerto Rico and an affiliate member of Edgehill United Methodist Church in Nashville, Tennessee. Carmen has studied at Seminario Evangélico in Puerto Rico and earned the doctor of ministry degree from Vanderbilt Divinity School. She is currently the international editor of **El Aposento Alto** *(the* Upper Room *devotional guide in Spanish) at the* **General Board of Discipleship.**

CHAPTER 1

What Is Death After All?

Ask the group to introduce themselves, giving their names and three or four personal beliefs about death and dying (without discussion). Or, use the game "Three Facts, One Lie." Of the four beliefs, one should be untrue. The rest of the group try to identify the lie. Afterward, invite all to tell why they decided to explore the topic of death.

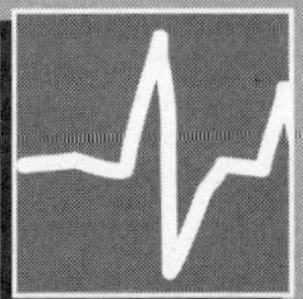

Have pieces of paper or index cards, markers, and tape or pins for each to write down the requested information. Let the group interact as they wish, but have them change partners after a few minutes, especially if they do not know one another well. Ask the whole group for their reactions and learnings during this exercise.

Have paper and colored markers available for each person. Have each person draw a vertical line down the center of

INTRODUCE YOURSELF TO THE PROCESS

This adventure into the topic of death is dependent on your willingness to talk about your views and experiences. You will read some information, but the most important part of the learning will come from discussions. In some exercises, only you will know your ideas and feelings. In others, you will be invited to express them to part or all of the group.

Do as many of the exercises as you can. Each is designed to get you deeper into the theme.

This chapter will help you have a general understanding of death as a physical, psychological, social, and religious event.

GET IN TOUCH WITH ONE LOSS

On a piece of paper, write your name and a personal experience with loss, such as an object, a pet, a relationship, an opportunity, a person. Tape or pin the paper to the right side of your blouse or shirt.

Then talk with the other persons in your group. Talk to those you do not know or, if you know everybody, to someone who has experienced a loss similar to yours. Ask about the losses.

THE LORD IS MY SHEPHERD

Psalm 23 is often read at funerals. For the next exercise, the leader will read Psalm 23 aloud. As he or she reads, list ways the psalmist describes God. Write each image on the left side of your paper. On the right side note ways you think God could help in times of need, based on the characteristics to the left.

WORSHIP

GROUP INTERACTION

DISCUSSION

Here's how you might start:

| shepherd | shall not want, provisions for different needs |

Say a silent prayer to God using at least three of the images/characteristics of God you noted. Ask God's help for the group as you explore the meaning of death and loss in life.

Use the personal discoveries about Psalm 23 in the following group discussion. Work in your group according to your leader's instructions.

YOU ARE MY SHEPHERD TOO

This resource discusses death from a Christian perspective. It includes references to books and experiences that support that view. These references also acquaint you with the tools God gives us to support and console us when we experience loss.

God provides consolation for us through the support of other people. But we usually need to feel comfortable before we are willing to talk about our losses or pain. Tell another group member about someone who was a good friend when you needed some help. (You don't have to report your conversation to the larger group.)

THE MEANING OF DEATH

In a discussion with the youth group at Hamilton United Methodist Church in Nashville, Tennessee, most of the teens said they never talk about death with their friends. Death isn't a popular topic, is it? You probably wouldn't talk about death at a party or in casual lunch conversation.

Still, death is an important subject. Sooner or later, nearly everyone is touched by the death of someone else; and everyone dies. Many of us think of dying as something that happens only to older persons—to someone else. But aging is only one of many reasons for death.

What images, ideas, or emotions come to mind when you think about death? Write in the space below some of your memories, feelings, or ideas. What do you think death is like?

Even though death is not a favorite topic for most, you wanted to be part of this group for a reason. Review why you decided to join. What are your goals as you participate in this group?

For a doctor, death is part of a sequence, part of the rhythm of life. Death is an inevitable event that occurs when body parts give out because of age, illnesses, or some other condition.

In our society, medicine offers new and better ways to sustain life. Thousands of researchers seek the cure to the most diverse kinds of medical conditions. In some cases, those medical conditions lead to death in a relatively short time, as with various cancers or with AIDS. In other cases, the body deteriorates progressively over a longer period of time.

Often life can be extended by medical means, such as special equipment, medications, and surgical interventions like transplants, which sustain a particular part of the body.

What illnesses or conditions that used to be fatal aren't fatal anymore?

Can you remember situations in which persons were kept alive by "life-support" systems for a long time?

Invite persons to talk about their goals (whatever they feel comfortable telling).

What do you know about decisions to use such systems or to disconnect them?

What, do you think, are the pros and cons of sustaining life artificially?

THE PERSONAL MEANING

So, medically, the functions of the body stop and the person dies. Seemingly, that is all there is to it. But is it? If that were all, you would not be in this group. There would be no point in discussing death.

Humanity has struggled with the idea of death for centuries. All major world religions try to address at least two basic questions: What is the meaning of life? What is the meaning of death? Even Hollywood, perhaps the last place some consider religious, has dealt with death.

Name movies you have seen recently in which someone died. Then discuss these points:

Is death central to the story? Is the movie an action/adventure one, with lots of blood and gore to make it "exciting"?

How is death portrayed? Does anyone seem to suffer? Does anyone mourn? For how long?

Do you think the deaths depicted were realistic? Why or why not?

Are these deaths interpreted in a religious way?

Death is also related to your pain when you lose a person you love or care about. Death creates the empty space you feel inside as you remember someone you will not see again. The absence of a person can change your life in many ways. Death can make you discover new emotions and experience life in unexpected ways. In fact, how you deal with the death of significant people in your life is how you will also deal with other significant losses in your life.

Death also affects the community (family, church, and other social institutions). A death can change a family's social situation: the father dies and the rest of the family cannot support themselves. Death can also be tragic or familiar to many persons, such as the murder of a well-known person or the suicide of a popular entertainer.

Distribute paper and pencils or pens. Have the group paraphrase the passage. Invite them to use the Bible dictionary and the concordance. Ask some to read their paraphrases aloud.

The book of Sirach is in the Apocryphal or Deuterocanonical writings considered Scripture by the Roman Catholic Church and some Protestant churches.

If you want to divide the chapter for a second session, close now with prayer and resume here next time. Begin a new session with a brief time to check on news and concerns of the group.

Ask the group to identify causes of death. A "hot potato" approach can involve everyone. Use a soft ball, or tie a tea towel into a knot. The person catching the "ball" answers, then tosses to someone else.

Read, then comment on the main points on this section.

O DEATH, HOW BITTER, HOW WELCOME

As Christians we have a long tradition to help us understand the meaning of death and life. Read the following passage; write in your own words its message about life and death.

> O death, how bitter is the thought of you
>   to the one at peace among possessions,
> who has nothing to worry about
>   and is prosperous in everything,
>   and still is vigorous enough to enjoy food!
> O death, how welcome is your sentence
>   to one who is needy and failing in strength,
> worn down by age and anxious about everything;
>   to one who is contrary, and has lost all
>   patience!
> Do not fear death's decree for you;
>   remember those who went before you
>   and those who will come after.
> This is the Lord's decree for all flesh;
>   why then should you reject
>   the will of the Most High?
>   Sirach 41:1-4a

ARE ALL DEATHS THE SAME?

There are different ways to die and various reasons for death. Age and its associated illnesses and consequences are major factors in the death termed "death from natural causes."

What other causes of death can you think of? With members of your group list causes or reasons for death.

Death occurs as part of the aging process. It can also come through long-term or short-term illnesses at any age, "an announced death." In an anticipated death, family and friends may find themselves providing for a patient's medical needs and other needs. They have to be prepared emotionally for positive and negative changes. In many cases, illness and subsequent death make long-term financial and emotional demands on families.

Sudden death, however, causes a different kind of grief. A car accident, gang or crime related deaths, the misuse of a gun—all make death a real possibility for youth.

Suicide, a major cause of death among youth, is included among sudden deaths. But suicide carries social and religious stigmas that make it different from other sudden deaths. Families may experience shame and guilt when a member commits suicide. Survivors may be rejected in their social and religious communities.

Not all deaths are the same. Every death has the potential to be equally painful, although in different ways and for diverse reasons—as you will discover as we continue the discussion of this subject.

On this or another page, write down beside each category the feelings and problems a person or family might have as they confront that kind of death. Then answer the questions that follow.

1. Death Due to Natural Causes

2. Announced Death

3. Sudden Death

Do you believe the feelings are the same? Or do you believe there might be different reactions and problems if the person died suddenly or after long illness?

DEATH AND SOCIETY

In the not-too-distant past most persons died at home. Doctors and hospitals often were not available. In some places today people still depend on natural remedies, healers, or nature to take care of illnesses. If such measures do not work, the person just waits for the end.

Today fewer people die surrounded by family members. Often people die in a hospital or a similar institution. While many family members may be involved in some way with the final illness, they might not be present at the actual time of death.

In the United States many people, urban youth in particular, are familiar with death because of violence in their environment. (Check out a TV or movie schedule for any night of the week. How many shows depict violence and/or violent death?)

Youth culture expresses many of its feelings and ideas about death and violence through music. Look at some popular songs that deal with death. Describe five points the songs make about death and violence in society today.

1.

2.

3.

4.

5.

What image(s) do you have of the United States and violence based on these songs?

How do you see violence affecting youth and being responsible for deaths in your age group?

DEATH AND THE CHRISTIAN FAITH

We need to see life and death from the medical, personal, and social perspectives. We also need to see how life and death have been regarded in the past and in other cultures. We shall not deal with that issue at length in this chapter, but the comparison may help us understand better why we stand where we stand and believe what we believe.

Different religions view death in different ways. Could you define, if asked, the Christian view of life and death? How do you know?

How have you learned about death from a Christian perspective? Who has helped you?

Most Bible scholars agree that human mortality was confirmed after the Fall (Genesis 3:19). As a result, no person escapes death. Life is connected to death; suffering, pain, struggle, and death are all part of human existence. But the Bible stresses the importance of building a spiritual foundation to support us in difficult times. When old age comes and death is near, it's good to know that one's life has been fruitful (Ecclesiastes 12:1-7).

But where are the dead? What happens to them? (These questions will be considered in more detail in Chapter 6.) The Bible offers many ideas about death. But the vision of death and what happens after death changed over the centuries in Israel. Just before Jesus' time, the prevalent hope in Jewish thought was for a future bodily resurrection for humankind, although many people did not believe in any sort of resurrection.

For first-century Christians faced with violent death because of their faith, the promise of a resurrection was the basis of their hope. Death by martyrdom meant entrance into a better life, life in Christ (Philippians 1:21-24).

Fundamentally, the Christian faith considers death an enemy conquered by the resurrection of Jesus Christ. His resurrection guarantees the resurrection of believers. Revelation 21:3-4 points to a time when there will be no death as the new era, the culmination of God's plan for this world, comes to its final stage.

Compare your view of death at the beginning of this chapter (page 9) with your view after reading and discussing the chapter.

BEFORE NEXT TIME

Get a notebook. Write down personal ideas and reactions to the discussions on death. For the next session think about the issues discussed today. Have you encountered any new ideas? What is the most significant idea you discovered today? How do you expect this new idea to be helpful to you?

Interview at least one relative or friend aged seventy or older (interview several if you can). Ask the person(s) to talk about traditions of the past related to death and funerals. Bring the information to the next session.

Bring pictures of yourself at different ages.

CHAPTER 2

Death Comes in Different Shapes

DECISION POINT

If there are new members in the group, introduce yourselves. Then review the information on losses from Chapter 1.

PULSE POINT

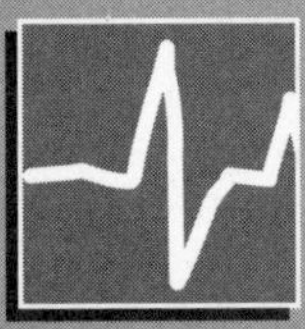

Discuss the questions in the text. Invite participants to check in with one another about personal activities or concerns.

GROUP ENERGIZER

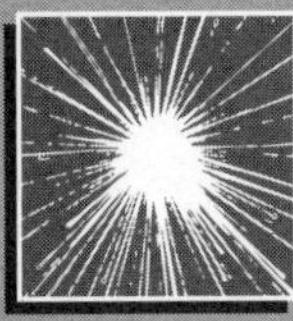

Form groups of three. Ask two persons to stand behind the third person. Encourage the third person to fall back into the arms of the other two people, but don't pressure anyone. Ensure the safety of each with cushions on the floor. Each person in the trio should have a turn falling back and being caught by the other two. Discuss as a group the text questions.

DEATH IS . . .

This chapter will help you understand that death is part of life and occurs in a variety of contexts, such as through the aging process, from illness, by accident, by suicide.

SO WHAT'S BEEN HAPPENING?

In the last chapter, you became better acquainted with feelings and attitudes associated with the losses in your life. What feelings, insights, changes of opinion, or new learnings about losses have surfaced for you?

What new thoughts or feelings about death came to you this week? If you feel comfortable doing so, discuss any ideas or memories you wrote in your notebook or journal this week.

I'M FALLING FOR YOU

Do a trust exercise. When everyone has had a turn, discuss your reactions. (I hope that as you get to know the other members of your group, you will feel comfortable talking with them about personal issues.)

How did you feel about letting someone catch you?

What ideas or feelings came to you as you let yourself fall back, without watching the people at your back?

If you didn't take a turn falling, what feelings did that choice elicit?

This exercise raises issues about trusting others. What, if anything, did you discover about yourself and your trust in others?

Before the meeting, prepare a picture or collage of people of different ages. Make this image the center of the space for worship time. Also in advance, ask one person to lead the group in prayer and another to read the Scripture.

Have the person who is to read the Scripture do so. Have the other lead the prayer. Sing or say together one of the hymns for funerals from your religious tradition.

DISCUSSION

Review the commentary in this section; pause to answer the questions throughout the text.

THE LOVE OF THE LORD IS STEADFAST

Read Psalm 103:13-18. Have one minute of silent meditation. Someone will pray for the group.

DEATH IS PART OF LIFE

As soon as we are born, our bodies begin to age. Death is in many ways the culmination of a process that began as soon as we came from our mothers' wombs. Does that make sense to you? The most dramatic way to see the changes is to compare the skin of a baby with the skin of people in their eighties.

If you brought pictures of yourself, show them and talk about physical changes in your life. What changes can you see?

What other signs of aging did you notice as you interviewed older persons?

What did you learn from the interview(s) about changes in attitudes toward death and aging?

Some scientists say that death comes as a result of wear and tear and the exhaustion of the body's resources. Others theorize that death is the culmination of a series of developmental stages as the body adapts to its external environment. As it ages, the body passes through stages, from development to maturity to old age to mortality. Death is the last event in a sequence beginning when life itself begins.

Whatever the theory, the older one gets, the greater the wear and tear on one's body. In old age, parts begin to wear out or break down, so much so that the general functioning of the entire body is affected. Eventually, major organs like the heart fail, and death occurs.

You probably have the same physical traits as one or both parents, such as the same build, hair color, height, and so on. What did your parent of the same sex look like at your age? If you strongly resemble one parent (even the parent of the opposite sex), what changes might you see in yourself when you are the same age?

Since you inherit your genetic codes, do you think your physical changes are fixed or completely predictable as you age?

What physical or psychological "script" do you see in your parents' generation? in your grandparents' generation? What factors contributing to that script are present for you? What can you control or change yourself?

WHEN DOES DEATH OCCUR?

Medical discoveries and the increasing sophistication of medical technology tend to blur the definition of death. With the assistance of life-sustaining equipment and other treatment, a person can be kept alive with basically only the brain working. The legal criterion for determining if death has occurred is whether the brain is functioning. (If brain activity has ceased, the person is legally dead.)

You are probably familiar with TV shows and movies that depict the revival of people who seem to have died. Such persons may be "clinically dead": no pulse, no breathing, no evident brain function. *Clinical death* refers to the brief period of time (less than four minutes) after the heart has finally stopped, during which resuscitation is still possible—although attempts are not always successful.

These are the crucial minutes generally portrayed in the movies and on TV. Doctors have to make quick decisions, depending on other conditions of the body. For example, if the person has terminal cancer, cardio-pulmonary resuscitation (CPR) might not be as crucial or as desirable as when the patient is young and in generally good health otherwise.

Have you or anyone you know considered your own wishes about "extraordinary measures"—medical and technical intervention that could sustain your life under very traumatic conditions?

One does not just "die." The period called "clinical death" is often preceded by what doctors term the *agonal phase*, just before death. This often momentary phase occurs as whatever constitutes life (call it spirit or soul) is extricating itself from the body. Some say the agonal phase is the final protest of the body against impending mortality. Physical signs include muscle spasms, heaving of the chest or shoulders (even a series of great heaving gasps), possible brief convulsion, sudden cessation of breath. One or more of these signs mark the agonal phase, the last phase of life before clinical death.

Jot down images of death and dying described in this section and in "Death Is Part of Life."

Compare these images and descriptions with the images and descriptions of death and dying in 2 Chronicles 21:8-20; Psalm 103:13-18; Genesis 25:7-8; 1 Kings 1:1-5, 9-11; 2 Corinthians 5:1-10.

SOMETIMES DEATH IS ANNOUNCED

Death can also come as a result of long-term or short-term illness. Cancer, heart disease, AIDS, and Alzheimer's disease are some of the "monsters" that announce death to a patient and his or her family. Illnesses like various kinds of heart disease lead to death, but with no predictable date. In other diseases, a doctor can anticipate the course of the illness and death fairly accurately, although some patients surprise everyone and outlive all expectations.

What, do you think, would be your initial attitude on hearing about your own terminal illness? What would you want your attitude to be?

Your attitude has a lot to do with how you handle stressful situations. Some persons, including terminally-ill patients, live until they die. Others begin to die when they hear the diagnosis. Families or persons coping with an announced death find it a constant, sometimes long-term, reality.

How do you understand those contrasting responses to life? What do you think you would do? What would you want to do? Why?

Have you known someone who was told he or she had a short time to live? How did the person react to the news? How did his or her family react?

Do you think death begins as physical limitations curtail one's opportunities?

The stress of taking care of a person for a long time depletes the emotional and physical energy of caregivers. This strain also affects the way they grieve, since grieving typically begins during the illness rather than at the person's death.

What signs indicate that a caregiver is "burning out"? What could you do to help?

DEATH MAY BE UNANNOUNCED AND VIOLENT

Accidental death prompts a special kind of grief and overall is the major cause of death for teens. Automobile accidents account for most of those deaths, but the level of violence in some schools and the availability of guns among youth mean that premature death is not far away from even the very young.

Have you known anyone who died accidentally? How did you react?

If you and the person attended the same school or church, what was the response there?

Did you attend the viewing or funeral? How would you describe that experience?

Youth are more familiar with accidental/sudden death than they once were. In a recent nationwide poll, more than thirty percent of the white youth and seventy percent of the African American youth personally knew someone who had been shot in the last five years.

In fact, gun use and gang-related violence are major factors in the death and injury of persons fifteen to twenty-four years old.

Accidental or sudden death causes a great deal of distress because we aren't expecting it. Typically we first feel shock and, if the death is violent, rage. Many people seldom think about death in relation to youth, but dangers in our society make sudden death a greater possibility than we may think.

Are there dangers or situations that make you fear for your safety? What are they? When do you encounter them?

Form small groups of three or four persons. Invite the participants to discuss Yummy's situation, adding these facts:

• Yummy was an extortionist and bully.
• He had been regularly abused by his mother and grandmother, who alternated custody. His father is in prison.
• At Yummy's viewing, neighborhood mothers brought their children to see what happens to kids who go wrong.
*• Yummy was "an average 11-year-old" his neighborhood. (See pages 54-63 of **Time** for September 19, 1994.)*

Encourage the group to move from this case to the broader issue of violence and death among teenagers and then to their personal situations. Do they know anyone in this kind of situation?

In pairs or trios, roleplay a situation in which one or more persons are comforting someone who has lost a friend or family member to suicide.

BIBLE STUDY

If you have time, use a topical concordance to look up instances of suicide in the Bible. What does the Bible say about those deaths? What doesn't the Bible say?

Some sudden and violent deaths seem even worse when they are steeped in notoriety due, for example, to the celebrity or age of the accused perpetrator. Even a quick glance at the daily newspaper or at tabloids in the supermarket checkout lane offers ready examples of both of these.

Equally tragic is the death of a young person. "Yummy" Sandifer was eleven when he died violently, only two weeks after he had killed a 14-year-old neighbor. In his short life, Yummy lived in one of Chicago's most dangerous neighborhoods and was an active gang member. He racked up twenty-three felonies and five misdemeanors in the last eighteen months of his life. Most likely members of his own gang killed him.

What else do you know about this case or the other "Yummy's" in our society? What responsibilities do we have to children and youth who seem destined for a violent life and an early death?

How do you protect yourself?

SOMETIMES DEATH IS CHOSEN

The grief of family members and friends is particularly painful when someone commits suicide. Even when suicide is considered as a sudden death, the feelings of grief are different, due largely to social and religious taboos and often unanswered personal questions.

Some families feel stigmatized by a suicide. They may feel guilt and shame over the event, as they and others try to make sense of what happened. Some might feel responsible, as if something they did or said might have caused the suicide. Suicide, according to some religious groups, leads to condemnation and eternal damnation. Family members thus might try to hide the cause or circumstances of self-inflicted death

for fear that their loved one would not receive a religious funeral or would not be buried in consecrated ground.

Often when a well-known person like a rock star or TV/movie idol dies accidently or commits suicide, fans mourn as if they have lost a family member or a close friend. Some persons have even considered suicide themselves.

DEATH IN REVIEW

Review the different types of death mentioned: announced, sudden, violent, chosen. In small groups create vignettes or scenes representing possible feelings or reactions of people hearing about a particular kind of death.

How would a close friend or members of the family react? How do you think you might react?

In what ways do you expect members of the family or friends to react? What do you expect of yourself? Are those expectations realistic?

What would you expect friends and members of the family to say?

BEFORE NEXT TIME

Write in your journal your thoughts about any death you can remember. Describe how you knew about it, who died, and what reactions or feelings you recall. If this death touched you personally, identify ways you received help as you confronted this loss.

If you have not yet talked to older member(s) of your family, try to do so this week. If family members are not available, visit a friend over seventy years old. Remember to ask these persons about their experiences with death.

CHAPTER 3

Is This Pain Ever Going to End?

PULSE POINT

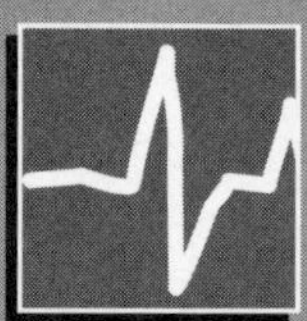

Invite group members to catch up with one another.

GROUP ENERGIZER

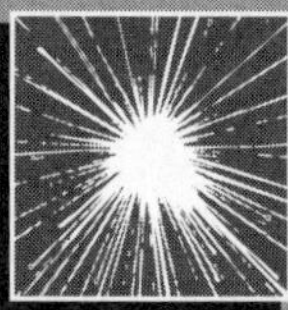

When everyone is done writing, collect, shuffle, and redistribute the epitaphs. As each person reads aloud an epitaph, omitting the name, ask the other group members to guess who wrote it.

GROUP INTERACTION

Have construction paper and markers available. Ask each person to write down any kind of loss and the associated feelings. Allow about five minutes for writing and five to ten minutes for discussion.

WORSHIP

Lead worship. Allow time for group members to think and pray. Have copies of the hymn available. Read the Scripture.

CATCH UP

Talk about discoveries you have made about yourself and your feelings. Include any journal entries you are willing to mention.

What traditions related to death did you discover in conversations with older adults? What did you learn about confronting death and grief?

This chapter helps you understand that a person's death affects us in different ways, depending on the significance of the person for us.

HERE LIES . . .

Write your own epitaph. Serious, humorous, whimsical—it's whatever you wish to say to "immortalize" yourself. Keep it for use in another chapter.

GETTING TOGETHER

Draw a patchwork quilt on a piece of paper. In each quilt square, write a short phrase or description of personal loss, like a person, a pet, an opportunity, or an object. Try to remember your feelings about the loss too.

Talk to another person about your discoveries. What feelings/emotions did you remember? What did your friend remember? How are you feeling right now?

WORSHIP TOGETHER

Think about someone significant in your life whom you have lost or could lose through death. Remember characteristics of this person that made him or her special to you. Recall moments you shared.

Think about yourself without this special person; then envision yourself getting on with life in healthy ways in spite of the loss. Pray silently for God to strengthen and sustain you in these times of sadness.

Sing together "Spirit of the Living God."

Hear the reading of Isaiah 40:27-31.

FEELINGS

Each of us reacts uniquely to losses. We react to death and to other significant losses in similar ways. But death affects us profoundly because of the intensely personal feelings it evokes.

What are some feelings associated with death mentioned in Chapter 1? Add other feelings about losses that you remember.

Some people feel uneasy about expressing certain feelings or think that they have no reason to feel sad. After all, death has happened before and will happen again. Nobody is justified in expressing despair under those circumstances, according to some.

The truth is that the healthiest way to deal with grief and sadness is to accept the feelings. Grief we express is grief we can live with. Grief suppressed rather than expressed will reappear in a variety of physical and/or psychological reactions that we cannot control.

DISCUSSION

Discuss your answers to the text questions about feelings. Review the ideas in the next two paragraphs in the text. Then discuss these questions:

★ Do you believe these ideas might be true? Why? What kinds of reactions do you believe grief can create?

★ Do you think some losses should not be grieved? Why or why not? Give an example.

★ What, do you think, is a healthy way to deal with grief? Have you ever realized that some physical distress was actually caused by repressed grief? Talk briefly about that experience.

BIBLE STUDY

Form small groups of up to five persons. Provide Bibles and commentaries on Second Samuel and John.

DEATH IN ANCIENT TIMES

Read one or both of these Bible passages:
• 2 Samuel 1:1-18 (the death of Saul and Jonathan)
• John 11:17-44 (the death of Lazarus)

These passages describe death in relation to two important figures in the Bible: David and Jesus. Notice the various emotions expressed by David, Jesus, and others in the family or community.

DISCUSSION

Give participants a few minutes for personal reflection. Discuss the questions in the text.

If you have time, discuss these questions:

★ *Jesus wept for his friend, even knowing that Lazarus was going to be well. Have you ever been very happy and very sad at the same time? What was it like?*

★ *David did not realize the Amalekite messenger was lying and that Saul had taken his own life (1 Samuel 31:1-4; 1 Chronicles 10:1-4). Have you ever "struck down the messenger" who brought you grievous news? What happened?*

DECISION POINT

If you have a short meeting time or wish to extend this chapter to a second session, break here. When you resume, begin with a brief prayer and invite group members to talk about insights or experiences since the last meeting.

DISCUSSION

In pairs, talk about an experience of being on an "emotional roller coaster" following a loss.

In a different pair, talk about ways you most often demonstrate grief, fear, and sadness. What feelings are easiest for you to express? Which are most difficult?

Use these questions as a guide for discussion:

What emotions are described? How are those emotions demonstrated? How did David and Jesus show their grief? Who else expressed grief? How?

How is the way most people in the U.S. express their feelings different from the way described in these passages? What is similar?

How do you feel about crying or other obvious expressions of grief? How do you feel when you see a child cry? a woman cry? an older man cry?

How would you behave and feel if you found out that a person you cared for had died?

Jesus expressed very strong feelings for his friend Lazarus, even after affirming the opportunity of resurrection (John 11:25-26). That Jesus wept for his friend assures us that these feelings are valid.

We can have a strong faith and still weep when we lose a friend or a family member. The closer a person is to you, the harder it will be for you to overcome the powerful feelings.

SOMETIMES WE FEEL, SOMETIMES WE DON'T

One characteristic of grief is that sometimes you feel sadness and sometimes you don't. Some days the feelings are so strong that you believe you won't be able to overcome them. At other times the feelings seem to be gone. Then suddenly, they're back.

Remember, too, that not all reactions are exactly as they seem. Some persons do not feel comfortable crying, although they are perfectly willing to express anger. Demonstrating one emotion while feeling another can be confusing for the person

Give each person a sheet of paper and a pencil or pen. Ask each to draw a circle in the center of the paper. Have the group write inside their circles the feelings they would express in front of others or would accept in others. Have them write unacceptable emotions outside the circles.

After the personal exercise, divide the large group into two or three smaller groups. Have the small groups repeat the exercise. The majority of each group must agree before writing down emotions inside or outside the circle. The team should be able to substantiate their choices/decisions. (You might also use this exercise in same-gender groups.)

If you have time, talk about possible consequences of labelling some feelings and exhibitions of behavior acceptable or unacceptable.

grieving and for those trying to comfort or offer care. In times of grief and stress, most of us struggle over which emotions to show and which ones to hide.

Culture shapes the ways persons express their grief and helps determine the range of emotions and behaviors socially acceptable or unacceptable. For example, in the United States many people from the white majority culture cry softly, if at all, at the funeral of someone close to them. But in some cultures public crying, shouting, and wailing are acceptable— although many persons in the US might find such public display of grief unacceptable. The range of acceptable emotions may become burdensome if you feel your emotions are unacceptable in your culture.

Create a visual description of emotions in grief that you consider personally acceptable or unacceptable. Write the acceptable expressions inside the circle and the unacceptable ones outside. Do one circle for your opinion. Create a second circle with your small group.

FEELINGS AND GRIEF

What are some of the reactions connected with grief?

- **Disbelief and shock.** These are often the initial responses when you learn that someone you love has died or is about to. The apparent lack of feelings and the sensation of emptiness are ways your body and mind give you extra time to adjust to the changes death causes. Shock can be expressed in ways that seem unusual, such as laughing at inappropriate times, not knowing or remembering what others have said directly to you, moving or doing things constantly, being subject to insomnia or excessive sleep, or becoming physically ill.

- **Denial.** Disbelief may turn into denial. You might want to believe that nothing bad is happening, has happened, or will happen.

- **Rage and anger.** Some people might feel angry at God, angry at the person who is leaving or has left them, angry for the burden of having to take care of a patient.

- **Guilt or regrets.** Guilt feelings may come from unsolved problems, conflicts, or other situations between the person who died and you. Sometimes we create our own guilt trip with the "If only . . ." self-recrimination. You might feel you were to blame for words you did not say or for promises you did not keep. You might remember conversations you wanted to have but didn't or ones in which you said things you now regret.

• **Depression.** Depression is the most common feeling in grief. Depression can manifest itself in a lack of interest in life or in other people, in eating too much or not wanting to eat at all, in wanting to sleep more than usual or in insomnia. One of the most troublesome aspects of deep depression is that the will to overcome it is precisely what depression masks or takes away.

• **Fears and panic.** The future, for a while, might look difficult, especially if the person who is dead or dying is a parent. The loss of a parent can be particularly devastating for youth. The fear of abandonment ("what will happen to me now?") is a normal reaction.

• **Physical symptoms and activities.** Some people are unable to stop "doing" when they feel sad. Their hyperactivity is a way of avoiding their sense of loss.

Think about the explanations of these reactions. Mark three reactions you feel or have felt most strongly in a time of grief.

Remember the quilt exercise at the beginning of the chapter? Think about a person identified in that exercise or in the worship experience after that exercise. What is or was your relationship with that particular person? Which of these reactions did you experience?

Do you feel there are issues you need or needed to talk about with that person? What would you talk about?

Write a letter, draw an image, or create a sign for the person. Acknowledge concerns, deal with unresolved issues, and express your care for that person—even if that person is gone. This sort of creative exercise can help bring a sense of closure, even if you are the only one who ever knows of it or sees it.

HELP IS POSSIBLE

Try to keep some important points in mind when you experience grief. First, the seven responses listed in "Feelings and Grief" are normal after a loss. Second, you may need help from others and will benefit from it.

Feelings are feelings. If we accept feelings of grief rather than deny or ignore them, we have a better chance of recovery. Even if we cannot believe that we will ever be free of these intense emotions, they will go away sooner or later.

Having recognized and named those feelings, you might need help overcoming the more serious aspects of your grief. Even though we say that "time cures all wounds," time helps only if you work with your grief. Though some strong feelings will disappear, you may need help dealing with others. A pastor, youth leader, family member, friend, or another trusted adult might offer the help you need. Your willingness to talk openly about how you feel and to trust your listener to keep your words confidential, without keeping harmful secrets, are important ingredients in successful grieving.

Even so, you might need more intensive help. A professional counselor can help you explore your feelings and memories. All of us might need that sort of help at some point in our lives.

As a special project, identify professional help available in your community. Are there pastoral counselors, psychologists, psychiatrists, social workers, and other professionals? Who are they? Are there mental health facilities? What kind? What services are offered? Gather the information by the next session.

HELP YOURSELF

We don't know when a crisis might affect us, but we can develop disciplines to help during hard times.

A marathon runner trains by following a proper diet, exercising regularly, and using the proper gear. What kinds of disciplines and activities, do you think, are comparable as spiritual preparation?

Accepting your feelings is probably the core of everything else you can do for yourself in life. If you are able to name your feelings and to recognize those you cannot handle by yourself, you have managed an important step.

Help yourself recognize your feelings by keeping a journal or notebook. You may write your thoughts or express them artistically. You can use a tape player or computer. A verbal or written journal is a way to observe yourself.

Another way to build your strength for times of crisis is to set aside time daily for prayer, meditation, and Scripture reading. These disciplines help build up your relationship with God as a friend.

The development of your personal strength plus support from the youth group, the church, and other friends can be of great value for you in times of need.

Identify any needs you have at this point.

Do you need to practice spiritual disciplines such as prayer, service, Bible reading, and so on?

Would you benefit from examining more closely your feelings about a particular person or situation?

Is there some unfinished or unresolved business you want to deal with?

Are you struggling with feelings of loss or grief that you want to talk about? Do you need a trained counselor to help you?

Think about or write down specific ways you can help yourself. Develop an action plan to follow through.

BEFORE NEXT WEEK

Remember to gather information about counseling resources in your community.

A way to remember someone who has died is to create a photo album or scrapbook and to collect mementos that celebrate and recall the person's life. If you can begin a book of memories before the death, so much the better. Consider starting this week.

How Can I Help?

WHAT TO DO?

Even though death is a natural part of the life cycle, it feels unnatural, and we don't always know what to do or say. This chapter will help you learn ways of supporting others who grieve.

SORRY, I CAN'T HELP

Play the game "I'm Sorry, I Can't Help." Afterwards, talk about your experience.

What do you think the purpose of the game is?

How silly did the excuses get? Which seemed realistic or plausible?

What does this exercise tell you about the walls we put up so we won't have to be involved?

What emotions might be behind our eagerness or reluctance to help others in sensitive situations?

What did you learn about yourself and your willingness to help others? about the importance of group work and mutual support?

WHEN DEATH GETS IN YOUR FACE

Choose at least two of the following case studies, and discuss the accompanying questions.

• Rob is 17. About ten years ago, doctors discovered he had a brain tumor. Rob had surgery and follow-up treatment and was apparently OK. About a year ago, Rob experienced some unusual numbness on one side of his body; the diagnosis was another tumor, but inoperable. Rob seems stable now, but his future is uncertain. His youth group, in solidarity with him, cut their hair short, the way Rob's was cut in the hospital.

How can people help one another in times of need?

Identify some ways Rob and his family might react to news of an inoperable tumor.

For each of those ways, what could be done to offer comfort or show support?

As Rob's friend, how might you help him?

If Rob were a member of this group, how could you support him?

• There has been a terrible automobile accident in your town. Five college students home for the Christmas holiday got together to catch up with one another. All were in a car when a drunk doing eighty hit it head on. Everyone died. Alicia, one of the passengers, was the oldest sister of your best friend, Norma.

How would you sort out your own feelings about what happened? (You need to do so before you try to help someone else.)

Do you know what you want to say to Norma? Do you know what to do? Can you talk to her about her grief, or do you have doubts because you don't know what to say? Talk about your reasons for what you decide.

If Norma were in your small group, what would you do? Do you think Norma would find the group supportive? Why?

Name several ways to support someone dealing with the sudden death of a family member.

• Paul and Nannette's father died last week after a lengthy illness. They had taken care of him for a long time. Sometimes they missed school and could not plan for or participate in social activities because they had to help at home. As a consequence, neither Paul nor Nannette has many close friends. Even though you don't know them too well, you think they might feel better if someone talked to them and showed concern.

What might Paul and Nannette need from you or your small group?

What might you do to show you care? Would you feel strange talking to someone you don't know well, especially in these circumstances? If so, what might help you feel more at ease?

Identify ways to show someone else you care even when that person is not close to you.

DECISION POINT

If you have a short meeting time or want to extend this chapter to a second session, break after the case studies.

When you meet again, begin with prayer. Then have group members talk about insights and experiences since their last meeting.

BIBLE STUDY

Have the tools for the study available. Do this exercise individually or in small groups. Ask everyone to work for five minutes listing inappropriate phrases and five minutes listing appropriate phrases.

Then record the phrases on a master list with inappropriate comments to the left, appropriate ones to the right. Have the whole group determine why any comments are inappropriate.

DISCUSSION

Briefly review insights and feelings from the case study activity. Refer to them as necessary.

• Consuelo and you have been friends since childhood. You know her immediate family and several of her extended family members. Consuelo's grandmother, who lived with the family, died recently. You would like to show your support to Consuelo, but you have some doubts about what would be appropriate. You don't know much about traditions Mexican families have about death.

What might be similar and different about the ways you and persons from another culture deal with customs and feelings surrounding death?

Should you say or do something similar to what you would say or do for another friend in this situation? Or should you treat Consuelo differently? Talk about your reasons.

When we don't know what to do, we often end up doing nothing for fear of doing the wrong thing. What might be the consequences of doing nothing? How might that compare with accidentally doing something wrong?

How might you help a grieving friend whose racial or cultural background is different from yours?

MY HELP COMES FROM GOD AND THE COMMUNITY OF FAITH

Using the Bible and a Bible commentary, study these passages:

• 2 Corinthians 1:3-7 (God consoles us in affliction.)

• Romans 12:15-16 (Rejoice and weep with others.)

• Job 2:7-13 (Job's wife and friends see his pain.)

• Job 4:1-11 (Eliphaz speaks to Job.)

Identify the things said, suggested, and done to someone facing a loss. Discuss all your discoveries.

WHAT CAN I SAY?

Refer to your list of discoveries and conclusions from the case studies in "When Death Gets in Your Face." Most young people I know feel uncomfortable about responding to someone dealing with the death of a family member or with serious illness.

List diversionary comments and activities you have heard, seen, or used yourself, such as, "Oh, don't say things like that"; looking all around; examining your fingernails or clothes; being silly.

"He looks so natural."
"I know just how you feel."
"She's with God now."
"If I can do anything, just call."

"Did she ever forigve . . .?"
"He had AIDS, didn't he?"
"Tell me all the details."

Roleplay a visit to a hospital or funeral home. One person is needing comfort; the others are visitors. Each group can do its scene for the others. After the roleplays, discuss helpful and unhelpful comments and actions.

If you have felt awkward about what to say to someone with a serious illness or what to say to someone who has recently experienced the death of a family member, don't feel bad. That awkwardness is not unusual; you're like most other people.

Because you feel uncomfortable, you might choose to be silent. You know the reaction: talking about anything else but the topic that makes you feel uncomfortable. Any sort of reference to death, direct or indirect, is followed by silence ("I don't wanna talk about it"). Or you change the subject ("Have you heard the latest CD from . . . "). But, your friend or acquaintance might need to talk or to hear something comforting when you launch into a new topic or lapse into silence.

You may fear sounding weird. You might want to say something, but the words don't come naturally. You may feel silly or fake mouthing the superficial stuff that is socially typical, but that's all you know to say.

Or, you may say more than you need to, by probing or making comments even when the other person shows discomfort. If your friend changes the subject when you mention the illness or death, leave it alone.

With two other persons, list words and phrases identified for each of these circumstances. Use a symbol for comments you think are helpful or appropriate and another symbol for inappropriate ones. Discuss your choices when you do not agree.

Are there phrases that might be used if modified? How might you improve them?

Now do the roleplay.

WHAT CAN I DO?

There are many ways to support others or show them you care. What kinds of support have you already identified? Consider the other person's reactions to the situation and to you as you try to help.

When you want to help a friend who has suffered a loss, try to find out something about his or her relationship with the person who died (without being pushy). You might find out indirectly. The death of an immediate family member is probably a significant loss, but the death of a close friend may be just as traumatic. Be careful about assumptions, however; they aren't always right.

How can you find out something about the relationship without being nosy?

What signs would help you understand underlying feelings about the person who died?

Remember, that, for better or worse, your friend will have specific feelings and memories related to the person who has died. The death of an abusive relative or a suicide might bring up a whole range of tormenting memories or even feelings of guilt and relief. We can't always know what secret fears or pains a death will provoke.

Also consider the circumstances surrounding the death. Young people might be angry with a parent or friend who had a lingering illness because of the stress of caregiving and disappointment over missed opportunities. In addition to feeling angry, a young person might feel guilty about that anger. He or she might feel abandoned and fearful about being left behind. Sometimes you won't know how your friend feels until you ask.

What clues indicate that a friend needs space or has too much space and needs company?

How do you know when a friend is too distraught to talk? How do you know that he or she wants to talk but is afraid to dump on you?

What else can you do to show you care?

GROUP INTERACTION

Reform the groups that worked on the case studies. Ask each small group to work out a caregiving plan and to be ready to present it to the whole group.

If your friend is willing to talk, just be real. Ask direct questions to help you understand your friend's situation, but don't push beyond what he or she can handle. Above all else, don't talk to anybody else about your conversation. Revealing deep feelings makes persons feel very vulnerable. If a friend willingly talks to you about personal feelings and experiences, you need to protect the confidence.

Keep in mind the stage of grief. A recent death might be more difficult to talk about than something that happened weeks or months ago. But let the other person know you are willing to listen and to help, according to his or her specific needs.

As a good friend, remember that sometimes, because of the intensity of the feelings, a friend might act as if he or she doesn't want to be around anybody else. Be sensitive to those desires, but make sure your friend knows you're there if she or he needs you. Your inattention might be very devastating for someone already depressed about a significant loss.

If your friend shows no interest in talking or if the person is someone you don't know too well, direct conversation is not always necessary. Instead, show you care by sending cards, asking the person to do something fun with you, or doing a favor without being asked. Sometimes just being together is enough.

Using the one of the case studies you discussed earlier and information from this section, create a plan to support a person who is grieving. Choose the role you want to take in this plan.

Indications of potential suicide include

• changes in eating and sleeping habits; nightmares
• feelings of worthlessness, hopelessness, isolation from friends or family, helplessness
• feelings of guilt, stress, anxiety; indecision
• fears about personal behavior, of hurting oneself or others; pessimism; irritability
• talk of suicide or previous suicide attempts; history of suicide of friends or family; having a suicide plan
• dependence on alcohol and other drugs
• recent losses (relationship, job or income); loss of weight or appetite
• loss of religious faith

Form small groups of four or five persons each. When the groups have completed their guidelines, discuss the questions in the text.

WHEN YOUR HELP ISN'T ENOUGH

Another issue to consider is the danger of suicide. As a friend, you are not prepared to provide the sort of help a professional can. But you might be the best person to notice if a friend is very depressed and possibly thinking about harming herself or himself.

You can ask your friend directly about any unusual behavior and try to convince him or her to talk to a professional, beginning with the pastor. If you think the situation is serious and that your friend is acting strange enough to try to harm himself or herself, you should talk to someone else—even if doing so means breaking a promise not to tell.

Keeping a confidence and keeping a secret are not the same. A troubled friend who admits to thinking about suicide or exhibits the warning signs may want you to promise not to say anything to anyone else. Keeping such a secret is not appropriate, for you or for your friend, when that person's health and safety are at stake. The pain of losing a friendship is nothing compared to the pain of losing a friend permanently.

Jot down your feelings and ways of reacting if a friend shows signs of considering suicide.

Create guidelines to use if you think someone is considering suicide.

What would you do? What would you say? Whom would you call for more help?

Read together Psalm 133. If group members have different translations of the Bible, ask each person to read one verse until the psalm is finished.

If possible, ask your pastor to talk about funeral rituals in your church. Ask him or her to explain the practices from a pastoral care perspective. Invite other professionals willing to give their time to explain legal and medical matters related to death. Ask these guests to come at the appropriate time.

WORSHIP TOGETHER

Read in unison Psalm 133.

Sing a hymn or song that conveys comfort to persons in distress.

Pray silently for the person on your left and the person on your right; then end with the blessing in Numbers 6:24-26.

BEFORE NEXT TIME

Remember your experiences with funerals and viewings. Think about embarrassing or difficult situations related to those experiences. Write down the most significant ones in your journal.

> We have received news that Rob, mentioned in the case studies, is no longer in remission and that the tumor is growing. We solicit your prayers for Rob, for his family, and for the youth of Hamilton United Methodist Church.

CHAPTER 5

Rituals and Death

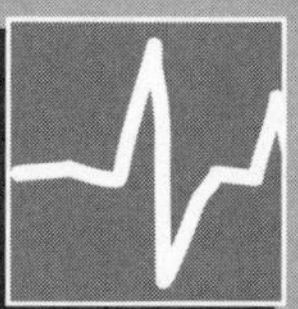

Talk together about what has been happening.

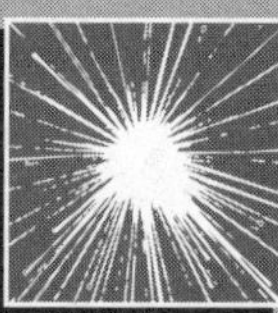

Play "The Nickname Game."

Review the epitaphs group members wrote (see "Here Lies . . ." on page 24).

What images are used?

Is there any message about expectations of heaven or an afterlife?

WHAT'S BEEN HAPPENIN'?

Talk with other group members about your feelings and ideas since the last meeting. You might mention things you have written or drawn in your journal.

MY FRIENDS CALL ME . . .

Mention a nickname or characteristic of yours, without an explanation. Then in a second round, tell how and why you received that name. (Careful about teasing!)

BEN FRANKLIN, PRINTER

Benjamin Franklin wrote his own epitaph:

> The body of
> Benjamin Franklin, printer,
> (Like the cover of an old book
> Its contents worn out
> And stript of its lettering and gilding)
> Lies here, food for worms!
> Yet the work itself shall not be lost,
> For it will, as he believed, appear once more
> In a new
> And more elegant edition,
> Corrected and amended
> By its Author!

Franklin wrote this while he was very much alive. He interpreted his life in images related to books and printing and introduced one way to begin thinking about his life and death.

LET'S TALK ABOUT RITUALS

This chapter discusses social rituals related to death and how such rituals can help one mourn.

In the past people were more willing to think about and plan rituals related to death. They knew that death could strike any time, at any age. But today preparation for and conversations about death are not as common.

We might feel death is too distant to worry about much. Or we trust the power of medicine and science to cure everything. We are not witnesses to death as often as our grandparents or great-grandparents were, for example, because most people now die in hospitals and institutions, away from family.

Death triggers intense feelings, which we sometimes feel uncomfortable expressing in public. We have been conditioned by our cultures. For many of us, crying in front of others is embarrassing! Customs surrounding dying, death, and grieving are determined in part by a particular time, a particular culture, and particular religious beliefs.

Spend some time with two or three members of your group describing what you know about viewings and funerals in your community. Write a description for someone from another country who has asked you to explain practices and traditions related to death in the United States.

What would you say to this person about what happens at a viewing? at a funeral? at a memorial service?

How would you explain these traditions or rituals?

What other observations do you have about attitudes and behavior of people who are in mourning?

What do you know about funeral and memorial customs in other cultures? Would mentioning those traditions to your friend from another country be appropriate?

What's a ritual? Suppose that each time a basketball player is on the foul line, he bounces the ball exactly seven times, then shoots. The bouncing is a ritual, something a person does every time he or she is in a particular situation. Rituals soothe us, providing balance and peace in turmoil and confusion.

Have the group identify common rituals, then read the examples of mourning rituals.

Has anyone visited the memorial or seen an AIDS quilt? Describe the experience.

Has any group member heard of a similar means of coping with grief?

Has anyone seen firsthand rituals in another country?

Ask the group to jot down feelings, not thoughts, that these experiences evoked. Ask why they think they had the feelings.

DEATH

WHAT ARE RITUALS FOR?

Within the last decade or so, United States citizens have created two significant social memorial rituals.

Since its dedication in 1982, millions have visited the Vietnam Veterans Memorial in Washington, D.C., and found and read aloud the names of friends and relatives who died during the Vietnam War.

The other ritual visit is to see the AIDS Quilt, first conceived in 1987. Each piece of the quilt, now the size of fifteen football fields, commemorates a person who has died from complications due to AIDS.

A California father whose teenage son died in a car accident learned that the tree his son had hit was to be cut down. He and his wife obtained the tree and, with the help of an artist, crafted a monument to fallen children. Working with the monument has helped him through his grief process.

When I went to Mexico in 1991, I experienced first-hand a centuries-old ritual memorial of the dead that is part of the traditions of Mexico and other Latin American countries. During the last week of October and early November, families remember their dead with altars on which are pictures of the deceased; favorite food of the deceased; and other symbols of death. Bakeries sell *pan de muertos* (bread of the dead) and in some places sugar skulls and chocolate coffins. Whenever possible, families visit the graves of deceased family members. In some small towns, special community activities remember the dead. As a result of these ritual activities, death is viewed as an integral part of life, and families feel spiritually connected to their ancestors.

Think about these rituals. They are not funerals, generally the rituals for the dead we are most familiar with.

DISCUSSION

Discuss the questions in the text.

DECISION POINT

If you have a short meeting time or want to extend this chapter to a second session, break here.

When you meet again, begin with prayer. Ask group members to talk about their insights and experiences since the last meeting.

BIBLE STUDY

Divide the group into three smaller groups. Provide a Bible dictionary and commentary. Invite the groups to read and research the passages, then present their findings to the whole group.

Discuss the questions.

REFLECTION

Allow time for personal reflection and journal entry. Invite personal comments.

ARE RITUALS HELPFUL?

What specific activities do you find helpful when you feel depressed?

How do you think rituals of any kind help families or a person feel better?

Why do you think particular gestures or actions help us accept our losses better?

When is a ritual not worth following? Why?

RITUALS IN THE BIBLE

Read the passage assigned to your small group:

- 2 Samuel 3:31-36
- Mark 5:21-24, 35-40
- John 19:38-42

Discuss these questions:

What rituals or practices are described?

What feelings are expressed? How do the people react to them?

Can you imagine yourself doing any of these rituals? Why?

Which action might better express your feelings about someone lost to death, a move to different home or a change in your relationship?

YOUTHSEARCH

Ask the pastor to go through the ritual with the group. If the pastor is not available, have copies of the funeral service available (see your hymnal or book of worship). Explain the service; answer questions.

Have any group members helped with funeral arrangements for a family member? Ask them to talk about the experience if they are comfortable doing so.

Has anyone attended a viewing? What was it like?

Have the group select several situations. Form teams, one for each situation. Have the teams work up their roleplays, then present them to the whole group. After the roleplays, invite comments.

RITUALS IN YOUR CHURCH

Discuss the funeral ritual used in your church.

Do you recognize different parts of the service? What questions do you have about any part?

WHAT TO DO WHEN SOMEBODY DIES

Most people in the United States die in hospitals. Sometimes, just prior to death, medical and legal questions must be decided: Will the family use extraordinary life-sustaining measures? Will organs be donated? Afterward, a physician must certify the cause of death. Sometimes an autopsy is required or desired. When these issues are settled, the body can be released to a funeral home.

At this point, the family's social rituals begin with plans for notifying family, friends, and business associates; for the viewing; and for the funeral. After the funeral, many families spend additional time together eating a meal. In some religious traditions, a memorial service is held some days after the funeral.

The viewing provides a time for closure (yes, this is real) and for supporting the family of the deceased. Be sensitive to the effect of typical social comments; avoid superficialities. If you knew the person, try to express what his or her life meant to you. If you know family members, indicate your willingness to hear and to support them as they struggle with their grief.

BE SUPPORTIVE

Are you unsure about what to say and do at a funeral or viewing? Roleplay some typical situations.

• Your best friend's mother, Mrs. Miller, died yesterday. You are sad too because you've been at that house a lot, and Mrs. Miller was always good to you. You plan to be with your friend today at the viewing. What should you say? How should you behave?

• Carlos, one your classmates, died in a car accident. Carlos's family is Puerto Rican. The whole class plan to visit the funeral home. How should you dress? What should you say and do as you talk to family members there?

• Your father's best friend died recently. The funeral is Saturday at your church. Your father expects your mother and you to go with him. What would be appropriate behavior? What should you say to the widow and other family members? Do you need to learn anything more about funerals in your church?

• Your father died yesterday, after a long illness. As the oldest son/daughter, you are responsible, with your mother, for funeral arrangements. What are you supposed to do? What should you say when persons visit or call?

• A classmate has committed suicide. The whole school seems to be in shock. The first viewing is tomorrow night, and most of the junior class will be there. What do you think will happen at the viewing? How will you help your grieving friends? What kind of help do you think you will need from them or others?

AT THE FUNERAL AND AFTERWARDS?

At the funeral and at the graveside, the family will be escorted to reserved seats. You can probably visit briefly for a few minutes before the service, if you couldn't go to the viewing. After expressing your condolences, find a seat not reserved for family. An usher may guide you.

After the funeral, you can continue to show concern by sending cards, calling on the phone, or simply inviting your friend or relative to talk at appropriate times. Remember, letting the other person know you care might be the best support you can offer.

YOU MEAN THERE'S MORE TO CONSIDER?

It's not too soon or morbid to think about how you want to die and what you want done after your death. You can decide about the options outlined on the next two pages *now*—and not have others decide for you in the future. Consider these items a sort of personal/legal checklist.

Sometimes there is a meal after the service that feels more like a party than a funeral. Has anyone been to a post-funeral gathering where friends and family members relax and unwind? What was that experience like?

Invite knowledgeable persons to talk about living wills, last wills, and organ donation. (Or get materials about such final plans.)

YOUTHSEARCH

REFLECTION

Do you have any instructions to add?

Living Wills

A living will addresses "extraordinary measures." Many hospitals allow or request patients to leave instructions about what to do if they cannot make decisions about treatment. Often families have to make treatment decisions for comatose relatives.

A living will can save a family legal and personal turmoil. You can prepare a living will any time in life. Consult a lawyer, who will help you create a legal document detailing exactly what medical intervention you will allow or not allow if you are unable to decide for yourself at the time. (A living will must be drawn up in accord with the laws of your state.)

Organ Donation

When you die, an organ you no longer need may save or enhance someone else's life. In some states the driver's license includes an organ donation consent form. You may need parental consent if you are a minor.

Last Will and Testament

A will can save a family anguish because it is a legal document stating exactly what the deceased person wants done with his or her possessions and assets. The more complex the family arrangement and financial situation, the more important the will is. But wealth is not the only reason to make a will. You need to say specifically what you want your family to do with things that are important to you. Make sure other persons know.

You need to consult a lawyer to meet the legal requirements of your state for both a will and a living will. Regardless of your age, consider making a simple document to provide your family clear instructions about your final wishes.

Funeral Instructions

When you die, what do you want done with your body? Some persons prefer a traditional cemetery burial. If you do, which cemetery? Others prefer cremation and specify what they want done with their ashes. Some donate their bodies for research.

How will your family deal with your wanting to discuss your funeral? How might you introduce the subject?

Have your parents or guardians discussed their own funerals? How can you help them make their wishes known?

Lead the liturgy printed in the text.

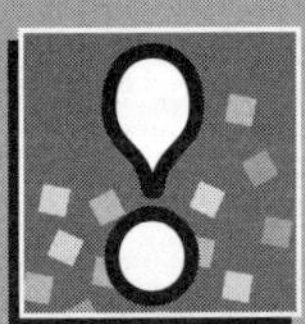

Chapter 6 covers biblical and theological foundations concerning death, which could be studied first.

If you are going to begin a new YouthSearch group dealing with death, decide whether you want to begin with Chapter 6; and consult current group members about inviting new group members to join you.

Does anyone know what sort of funeral or memorial service you want? What kind of music or visitation arrangements do you want? Should the service include the reading of particular Scripture or something else meaningful to you? If your preferences are unusual, discuss them clearly while you can.

Thinking about and planning your own funeral is not fun, but it can help you and your family in more than one way. It helps you find out what you believe and feel about death and focus on what is important to you. Remember that the family left behind will make the final arrangements; knowing your wishes will make their decisions easier.

WORSHIP TOGETHER

Read Psalm 130.

Read together this prayer of thanksgiving:

> God of love, we thank you for all the happiness with which you have blessed us even to this day: for the gift of life; for our home and friends; for health and strength; for work, and nature, and beauty; for our baptism and place in your church with all who have faithfully lived and died. More than all else we thank you for Jesus who knew our griefs, who died our death and rose for our sake, and who lives and prays for us. As he taught us, so now we pray. (*Continue with the Lord's Prayer.*)

Read Romans 8:35-39.

Sing together the hymn "Precious Lord" or another hymn that brings comfort.

YouthSearch

The Christian Hope: Death Is Not the End

PULSE POINT

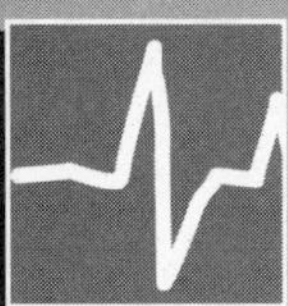

Discuss some of your in-depth explorations and personal revelations.

GROUP ENERGIZER

Have colored markers, construction paper, scissors, and glue for the notes.

GROUP INTERACTION

Form same size groups. Include in the litany learnings or discoveries the group are grateful for. List people and issues for prayer.

Ask one person to lead the litany and another to lead the prayer.

BIBLE STUDY

Pair off. Ask each team of two to study and discuss all (or most) of the passages. Give each team a psalm. Have concordances, Bible dictionaries, and commentaries so persons can find other Old Testament texts about death. Post all discoveries.

CHRISTIAN HOPE

This chapter presents the teachings of the Bible and the church about death. Although you have studied the Bible in each of the other chapters, this more extensive study is the basis of the Christian understanding of death. Jesus' death and resurrection is the center of our faith and our hope as Christians.

A GIFT FOR YOU

Prepare personal notes shaped like presents, one for each group member. Tell each person how he or she has made a difference for you during this study.

PREPARE FOR WORSHIP

Work in two groups on the closing worship. One group will do a litany of thanksgiving; the other will prepare for the closing prayer of petition. Remember, as much as possible, those struggling with death or illness in their family or circle of friends.

When the litany of thanksgiving is finished, write it out on poster paper. Post it where everyone can see it. Leave space for new items. Post the prayer list, allowing room for petitions you may want to add during worship.

DEATH IN THE OLD TESTAMENT

First Samuel 28:3-19

Many other cultures during the early history of Israel accepted communication with the dead as normal and possible. The story in 1 Samuel 28:3-19 represents that position, but clearly indicates God's displeasure with it. Nations surrounding Israel might have believed in communication with the dead, but Saul and the Hebrews should have known not to try manipulating the future or God by such means.

What is divination? What are soothsayers, augurs, and sorcerers? What is the allusion to passing through fire?

Do you think God "takes away our breath" when we die? Support your answer.

Do you think that when you die you will be reunited with deceased family members?

What is the essential attitude of this passage? (encouraging, cynical, realistic, or what?)

What does each psalm say about death? What does each say about the relationship of God, human beings, and Sheol? Who goes to Sheol?

Deuteronomy 18:9-14

Later biblical texts indicated specific prohibitions against any contact with the dead. Read Deuteronomy 18:9-14. Comment on the instructions concerning ghosts and communication with the dead.

Verse 12 says any attempted contact with the dead is considered an abomination. Contact with the dead is placed in the same category as making human sacrifices and worshipping idols.

Do you see any relationship between the prohibitions in the Bible and cultural influences from other nations? What danger, if any, do you see in trying to communicate with the dead?

Psalm 104:27-30

The first understanding of death for Israel was that in death people return to dust. Human beings were like animated bodies, with no life independent of God. A person died because God took back the life-sustaining spirit. Read Psalm 104:27-30 (note especially verses 29 and 30).

Genesis 25:7-8

Later, death was interpreted as the first step in going back to one's ancestors: Abraham died and "was gathered to his people." There was a special, communal bond between God and Israel. When someone died, that person returned to the family or tribal ancestors.

Ecclesiastes 9:1-10

As Israel developed the concept of death, a more personal interpretation became acceptable. Death did not involve just the nation or the family. Death involved a disruption of the relationship between the person and God. What does Ecclesiastes 9:1-10 say about life? about death?

Psalm 16, Psalm 49, Psalm 73

At a later stage, God's power is interpreted as going beyond life and death. Some psalms reflect the belief that God can help the just overcome the power of Sheol (the place where the dead go). Sheol, according to some scholars, was a place for the ungodly, not necessarily for the just. Portions of Psalms 16, 49, and 73 reflect this belief.

How is the concept of life after death changing? Do you think all the concepts are true? Are resurrection and life after death "later inventions" of God, or were they just unknown earlier?

Discuss the summary questions. Review posted findings.

REFLECTION

This activity is optional. *See 2 Maccabees 7:6, 9, 11, 14, 22-23, 28-29. (The full, gorier story is in 4 Maccabees, chapters 8–12.)*

What do the verses say about life after death?

What kind of test could your faith withstand?

DECISION POINT

If you have a short meeting time or want to extend this chapter to a second session, break here.

When you meet again, begin with prayer. Encourage comments about insights and experiences since the last meeting.

"Resurrection" Passages

Much later, the idea of a general resurrection of the dead began to take shape (Isaiah 26:19; Daniel 12:1-3). Eventually people began to believe that at some point after death the dead would be resurrected and judged by God. The Bible often refers to this "resurrection" as the Day of the Lord (see Joel 2:1-2). Read the three passages mentioned in this paragraph. What do they say about resurrection?

What have you discovered as you read the Scripture passages? What is new to you? What do you see as important to you personally?

What new ideas do you have about what happens when you die?

BETWEEN THE TESTAMENTS

As Greek ideas about body and soul began to influence Jewish thought, new ideas began to develop about resurrection. The soul, according to those new ideas, was immortal; but the body was not. It was subject to death, to decay. These Greek ideas, among others, influenced Roman thought after Rome conquered Greece in 146 B.C. and absorbed Palestine into the Roman Empire.

Persecution during the Greek and later Roman occupations of Palestine no doubt disposed Jews to hope for and believe in vindication after death, if not in life.

If you have a Bible with the Apocrypha, look at 2 Maccabees 7 for an account of the torture of a mother and her seven sons because they would not renounce their faith or engage in pagan practices.

FOCUSING ON WHAT YOU BELIEVE

By Jesus' day there were four basic positions in Jewish thought about death and the afterlife. The Sadducees believed there was no resurrection and no afterlife. The Pharisees believed in a resurrection of the body at the Last Day. The third position was that the soul was immortal. The fourth was that although the body was not raised, people would exist in a state somewhat like that of angels.

The diversity of beliefs about death and afterlife continues among Christians today. Although the Bible gives us clues, it does not clearly state exactly what happens after death. I suspect that the biblical writers were aware that there will always be a limit to the knowledge we have of life after death. Death is still a mystery for human beings.

WHAT DO YOU THINK?

Develop your own creed about death and resurrection. Write only about what you can believe in based on your research to this moment. Keep in mind the following questions as you write:

Do your actions and beliefs depend on whether you think death leads to nothing or leads to a new life?

In what specific ways do your beliefs about life (or nothingness) after death influence your life now?

Has anything you have learned from the Bible influenced what you believe? If so, how?

DEATH IN THE NEW TESTAMENT

The death of Jesus Christ and God's raising him from the dead are central events of the New Testament. Our belief in the power of the death and resurrection of Christ is the basis of Christianity. And our belief in the Resurrection puts the life and death of all humanity in a new light. Paul affirms that unless we believe that God has raised Christ, our faith is vain (1 Corinthians 15:12-19).

Early Church Views of Death

Against the background of the four Jewish positions on death and afterlife, the early church began to develop its own ideas of death, life, and resurrection. Find the following passages in your Bible. In the space after each reference, paraphrase or interpret the meaning you give to each passage. Consider what each says and what difference it makes in your life if you believe it.

• Luke 20:27-40

• Matthew 25:31-46

- First Corinthians 15:1-11

- First Corinthians 15:35-44

- First Corinthians 15:50-55

Symbols of Power

Death's power over humanity was changed through the death of Jesus Christ. For Christians, the death of Jesus Christ was the beginning of a new era, effected by the power of his resurrection (1 Corinthians 15:54-55).

The presence of Jesus, in this life, and his resurrection are symbols of the power of God to defeat death. The teachings, miracles, and resurrection of Jesus show that the will of God for all creation is life. God offers an abundant life to all who believe. An abundant life is not without problems or pain, though it is marked with "righteousness and peace and joy in the Holy Spirit" (Romans 14:17) and the inner assurance of God's presence in and even beyond this life.

For first-century Christians, persecution was common, and violent death was always a possibility (see Acts 7:54-60). Baptism was associated symbolically with death to an old life and the beginning of another (Romans 6:3-5; 2 Corinthians 4:11; Revelation 12:10-12). So physical death in that context meant the entrance into a better life, life in Christ, and freedom from persecution—but also entrance into the eternal peace of God (see Philippians 1:19-26).

Read aloud Luke 24:13-35. Give persons time to think about the story. Invite comments on the experience.

Have additional paper available. As group members revise their creeds, invite them to think about what they have learned so far.

Discuss these questions and those in the text:

★ What important discoveries have you made during your YouthSearch group experience?

★ What wisdom is there in death?

★ Has learning more about death from physical and faith perspectives influenced your attitudes about what is important in life? If so, how?

★ What is the most important thing you will take from this learning experience?

Walking With Jesus to Emmaus

Get comfortable and listen to Luke 24:13-35. Imagine yourself as part of the action.

Which character do you identify with? Why?

Which part of the story is most interesting to you?

What would you ask or say to Jesus?

REVIEWING YOUR CREED

Look again at the creed you wrote earlier. Refer to posted comments from group activities and think about the discussions. Remember the New Testament teachings about life, death, and resurrection; and keep in mind the importance of your belief for your life. Does it make any difference to agree with Paul or with the stories in the Gospels?

Share your revised creed with the rest of the group if you feel comfortable doing so.

DEATH FOR US TODAY

This resource does not offer a historical review of various concepts about death. But we do need to consider the idea that death can be a teacher of wisdom.

How can death teach us wisdom? Not by making us afraid of life and responsibilities or by making us cynical and irresponsible. Death is final; there is no more time. Death is common to all living beings on earth. It is, in fact, the great equalizer: everyone must die. Nobody can run away from death.

So, how is death a teacher of wisdom? We all know that we will die. But we do not know when and how we will die, so every minute is important and precious. We are responsible for using that precious time, aware that it is a gift in itself.

Because I know that I will die, I must reject illusions about the eternity of my human efforts. The poor and rich, the famous and infamous—all will come to the same end; wealth and fame may die too. I know that everything that breathes must die. I must therefore use my time wisely, committing myself to beliefs and actions that have profound, perhaps eternal, value.

Do these comments make sense to you? Which ideas do you see as useful for your own life at this point?

Decide who will lead worship. If you want to celebrate Communion, invite the pastor. Integrate the litany and prayers into the service. You might lead the benediction.

Provide large blank index cards, or make up a short questionnaire.

WORSHIP AND CELEBRATION

Update your litany if you need to and post it where everyone can see it. Add prayer requests or issues for celebration to the prayer list posted earlier.

Remain silent for a few moments.

Say the litany of thanksgiving.

Write down or comment on the meaning of this group for you. Have you been able to reach the goals you identified at your first meeting? Was there a particular activity or idea that was important to you during this time with the group? Why was it important? What new visions or possibilities do you see for your personal growth as a result of this study?

Sing together "Hymn of Promise" or another resurrection hymn or song.

Join in the prayer of petition and close with a benediction.

EVALUATION (OPTIONAL)

Write, on one of the cards provided, any comments or recommendations for the leader for future Youth-Search groups studying *Death*.

Send an evaluation to the editor if you wish.

> Editor of YOUTHSEARCH: DEATH
> The United Methodist Publishing House
> P.O. Box 801
> Nashville, TN 37202-0801

The YouthSearch Group Experience

used in a variety of settings. Although it was not planned for use in Sunday school, you may choose to adapt it for the length of time available on Sunday morning. "Bringing YOUTHSEARCH to Sunday Morning," on page 55, will help you adapt the material for your group.

A YouthSearch group is composed of youth and an adult leader. They come together to learn about a particular issue and to grow in Christian faith and discipleship. Your group will meet on a regular basis. The sessions will be informal; they will not feel like schoolwork. Creating an atmosphere of honesty, openness, and trust will allow the youth to struggle with their own spiritual development. In fact, a YouthSearch group may become a miniature community of faith as the members of the group support and encourage one another, emphasize their relationship with Christ, and become more aware of each person's spiritual development.

Your YouthSearch group will be unique. The youth who participate will contribute their own perspectives, feelings, experiences, yearnings. They will work and learn together in distinctive ways.

As we developed YOUTHSEARCH, we imagined youth and adults exploring a crucial area of daily life and discovering a spirituality that would strengthen their decisions and actions. Every volume of YOUTHSEARCH focuses on a specific concern that can be explored in six or more sessions. It is designed for small groups and for time periods of ninety minutes. The book can be

Many YouthSearch groups create and adhere to a covenant that specifies the purposes, the hopes, and the expectations of the group. If the participants in your group decide to create a covenant, be sure they review it often so that it continues to call them toward a common faith and life.

Bringing YOUTHSEARCH to Sunday Morning

Although YOUTHSEARCH was not created specifically for Sunday school, it can be adapted so that it provides a terrific resource for small groups of youth who meet on Sunday morning. If you decide to use YOUTHSEARCH on Sunday morning, be creative and flexible in adapting it for your group.

The most significant change you make will be to adjust sessions so that they fit the time avaliable to your group. YOUTHSEARCH is designed for ninety-minute sessions, but you may have only thirty or forty-five minutes. Pay careful attention to the Decision Point icons. They will suggest an appropriate place to divide each chapter into more than one session. Use the Decision Point to help you divide the chapter into shorter sessions that will work for your group on Sunday morning.

When adapting YOUTHSEARCH for your group, keep in mind the basic parts of each session. Every time your group meets you will probably want to include an opening activity that will help the youth feel at ease, Bible study, discussion, time for reflection that will encourage the youth to apply what they have learned to their lives, a closing activity, and a time to look ahead to the next session.

By using the icons and planning carefully, you can use YOUTH-SEARCH to open the door for lively, stimulating discussions about issues that are crucial for the youth in your group.

Using YOUTHSEARCH on Sunday morning will provide opportunities for the youth to help lead sessions. Group members will develop a sense of community when they practice openness, hospitality, and candor during YouthSearch meetings. Participants may not attend every Sunday; so during every session, emphasize the need to call people who were absent and to encourage their participation.

YouthSearch groups offer participants an environment in which to explore critical life issues, to experience the life-giving Christian community, and to develop skills that are crucial for their faith. Thoughtful planning will create an atmosphere of friendliness and mutuality that can turn Sunday morning groups into communities of caring and learning.

Starting a YouthSearch Group

All you need to start a Youth-Search group is interest and investment. Youth are more likely to get excited about topics that relate to areas of their lives that are of interest and concern to them. Selection of a topic and careful preparation will show the members of your group that you are interested in them.

Preparation is crucial. YOUTHSEARCH is designed to be used with small groups of people who have come together to learn and to grow in faith.

To start a YouthSearch group,

▶ begin by reading *Start Up!: Preparing to Lead Your Small Group*, the first volume in the YOUTHSEARCH series. *Start Up!* offers practical suggestions for leading a small group. It will help you develop your skills and build your confidence.

▶ begin with one of the books in the YOUTHSEARCH series. Read the articles, such as this one, that appear in the back of the book.

What's the right size for a YouthSearch group? The ideal size of a small group is between four and twelve people. If more than twelve youth are interested in participating, invite them to form more than one group. If they prefer to stay in one group, be aware that some youth may feel uncomfortable talking openly in a large group. Plan sessions that include activities for smaller groups.

In many churches, small groups provide the setting for study, fellowship, mission, and worship.

Small groups are formed to encourage interaction, to prepare people for membership, to include new members in the life of the church, to explore difficult life issues.

Work with the participants to make decisions that will affect the size or the personality of the group. Ask them to consider issues such as creating a new group, inviting new members to join the group, or changing its purpose.

Youth respond to personal invitations. Follow up invitations with phone calls or notes to confirm their participation. When you invite youth to participate, be sure to tell them the topic, the names of other group members, and meeting times and places.

Emphasize the importance of attending each meeting of the small group. Unavoidable emergencies may occur. Make note of absences; call group members who miss a session and let them know they were missed.

Before you start a YouthSearch group, be sure you know the answers to these questions:

▶ Who's going to lead the group or groups?

Will you be leading all the sessions? Will you and another leader be present at every session? Will you recruit leaders who will learn to lead their own groups by working first with you or another experienced leader?

▶ Where will your group meet?

Meeting at the church has advantages and disadvantages. Would your group prefer to meet in someone's home? If you meet away from the church, what arrangements for transportation will you make? If you decide to meet in a person's home, how will you ensure that interruptions and distractions are kept to a minimum?

▶ How will you get everyone a copy of YOUTHSEARCH before the first meeting?

The members of the group may want to look over the book before they meet. During the first meeting, invite the participants to become familiar with the book's topic, purpose, and contents.

▶ Will your group be open to new members or will other people wait for a new group to be formed?

We suggest that you encourage the youth to join the group during the first or the second session. If other youth want to be part of the group after the second session, ask them to wait until another group is formed.

Your group may work through only one book in the YOUTHSEARCH series. Or you may design your educational program around the topics in YOUTHSEARCH. First impressions are important. Be sure to prepare carefully for the first sessions with your new YouthSearch group.

Tips for Lively Discussions

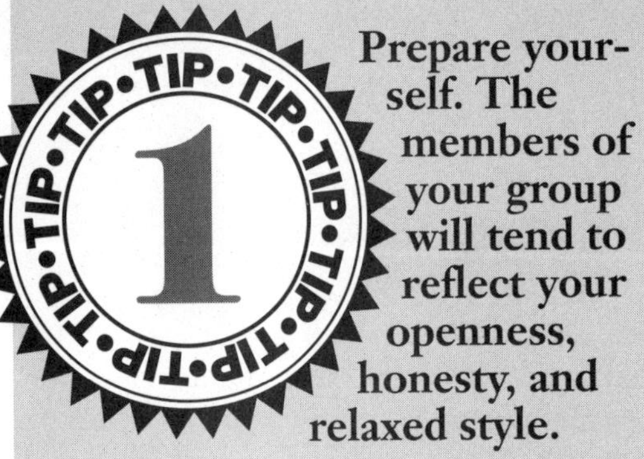

Prepare yourself. The members of your group will tend to reflect your openness, honesty, and relaxed style.

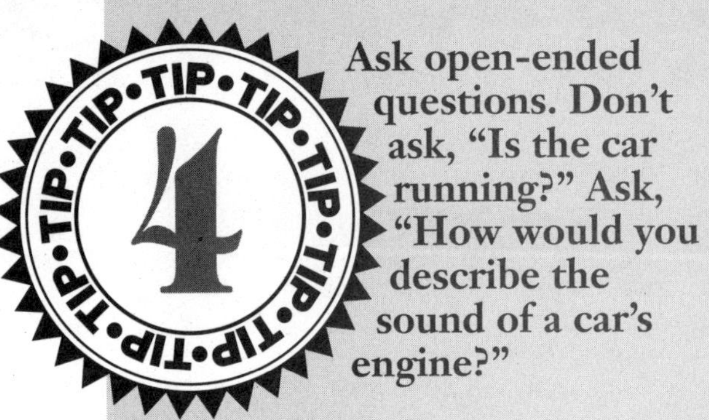

Ask open-ended questions. Don't ask, "Is the car running?" Ask, "How would you describe the sound of a car's engine?"

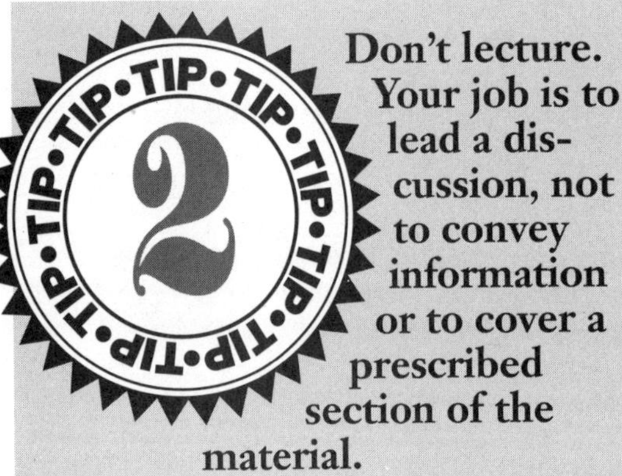

Don't lecture. Your job is to lead a discussion, not to convey information or to cover a prescribed section of the material.

Ask follow-up questions. If someone in the group makes an interesting statement or offers a unique perspective, ask, "Why do you say that?" or say, "Tell us more about that."

Know the members of your group. Be aware of their concerns, perspectives, and experiences.

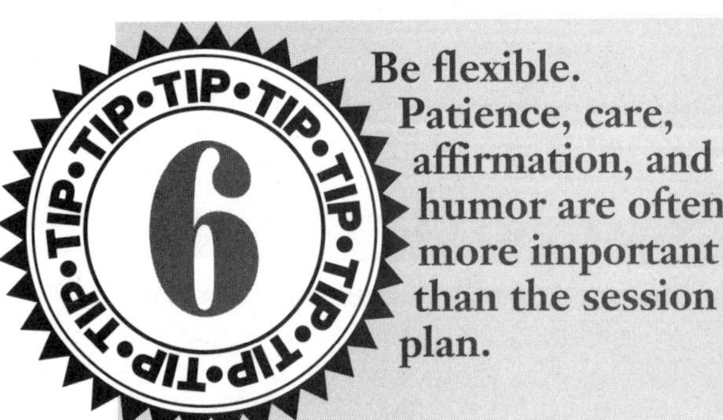

Be flexible. Patience, care, affirmation, and humor are often more important than the session plan.

TIP 7 — Encourage the participants to talk with one another rather than with you. Direct the conversation—for example, when one member of the group comments, ask another person to respond.

TIP 8 — Trust your group. Let the group lead discussions. Let the group set the agenda. Your task is to serve the group and to facilitate the group's discussion.

TIP 9 — Monitor the conversation. Don't try to do everything. Use the options offered in YOUTHSEARCH to create a balance between taking on too much of the topic and doing too little.

TIP 10 — Don't be afraid of silence. Sometimes people need time to think. Help the group feel comfortable with silence by saying that quiet times are natural and that they allow people to think through what they want to say.

TIP 11 — At any time, an individual may choose not to participate in the discussion. People who need time to think about a response or who choose not to comment should be able to say, "pass," without feeling uncomfortable.

TIP 12 — Evaluate. Ask the members of the group what is helpful to them and what needs to be improved.

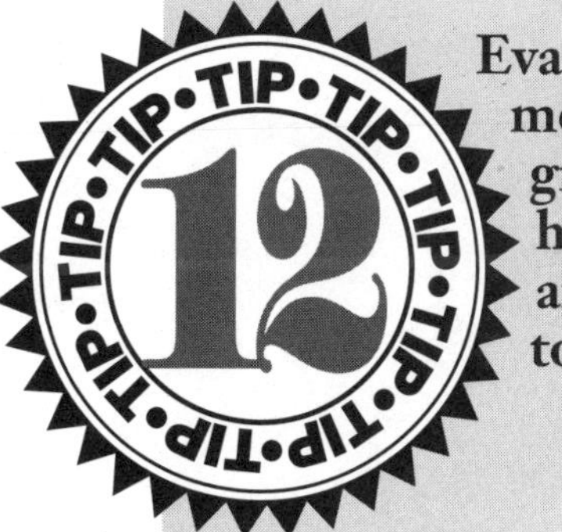

Taking Your Group's Pulse

How can you tell if your YouthSearch group is healthy? We determine if a person is healthy by taking his or her pulse and listening to his or her heart. Evaluating the vitality of a group is perhaps more subtle, but there are ways to determine the health of your group and ways to strengthen its heartbeat.

Check the group's pulse at the beginning of each session. Pulse Point icons identify times to assess the group's feelings. At the end of each session, encourage the participants to complete the chart on page 61. Then begin the next session by asking volunteers to report their responses. If you have more than six sessions, photocopy page 61; and give each participant a copy.

▶ Keep the group aware of its covenant.

At the beginning of each session, invite the participants to recall the commitment they have made to the group. During your review of the covenant, you may detect waning or shifting interest. At this point, members of the group may choose to change the covenant so that it more clearly reflects their concerns and expectations.

▶ Pay attention to the atmosphere of the group.

Jesus created an atmosphere in which the disciples knew that they would be accepted and loved even when they failed. When discussing tough issues, some members of your group may wonder if they will be accepted if their positions are different from those of other people in the group. Be aware of discomfort, hesitation, or uncertainty.

▶ Keep an eye on absences or tardiness.

If a group member is repeatedly late or absent, he or she may feel uncomfortable with what's happening in the group. Regular absence and tardiness hurts the group. Respond immediately; talk to the person; find out what's happening.

▶ Unpack a session or two with a person or two.

Immediately following a group meeting, ask one or two participants to talk with you about the session. Ask: What was exciting? boring? interesting? Listen to what they say; and in the next session, make changes that reflect their concerns.

YouthSearch Pulse Record

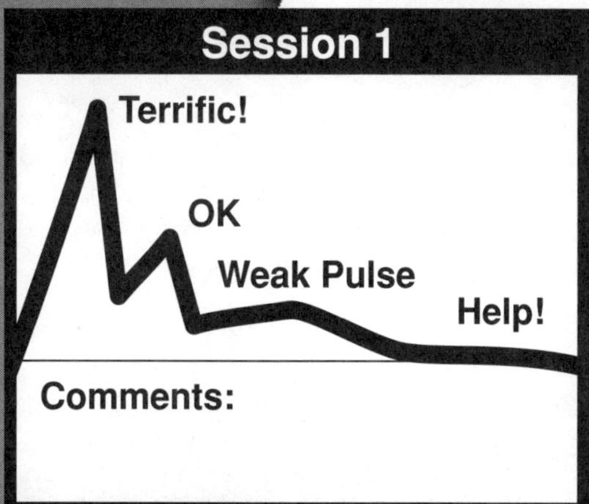

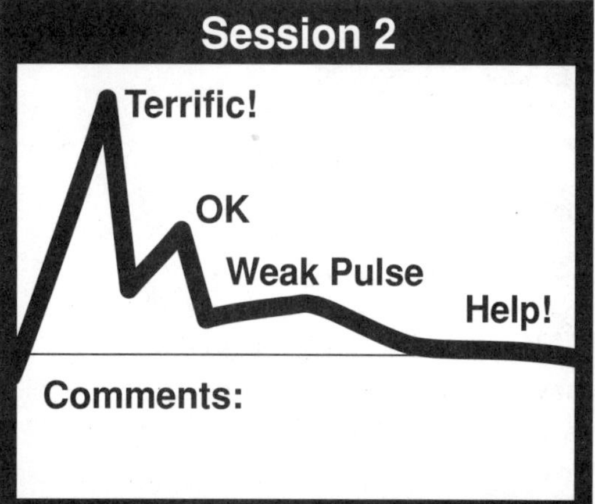

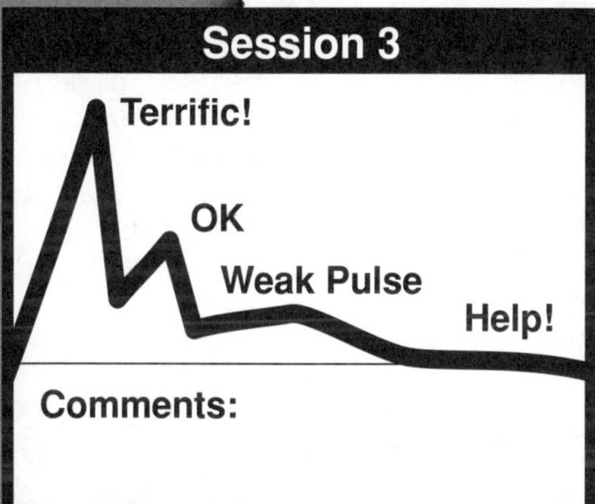

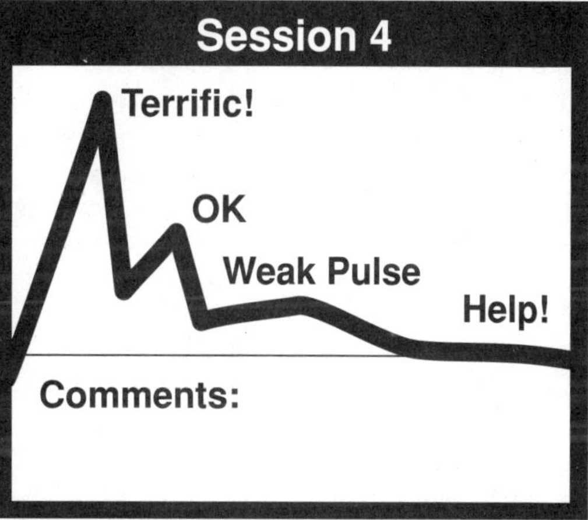

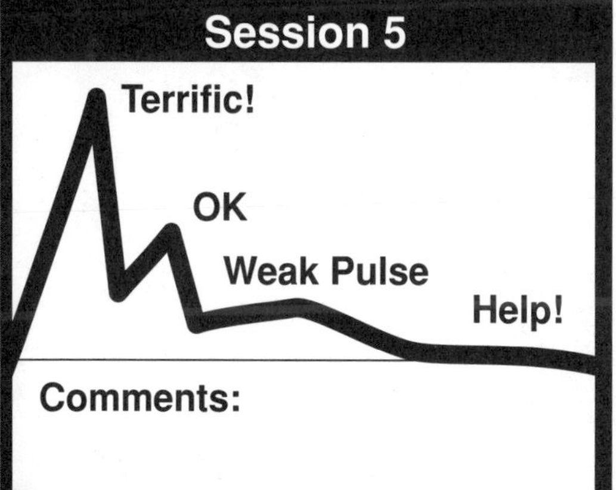

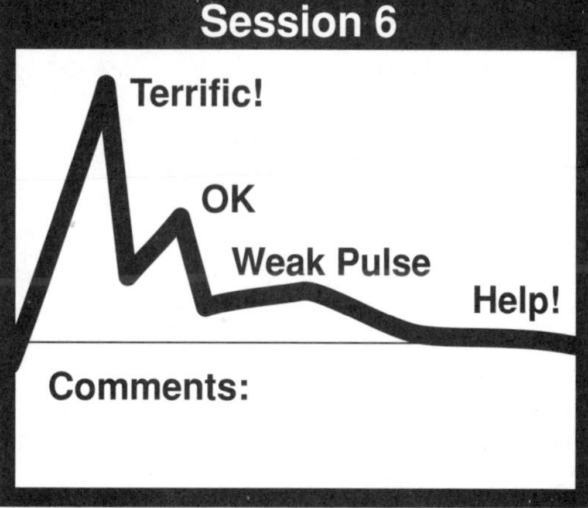

Dealing With Group Problems

People bring energy and excitement to a group. They also bring their own ideas and their own unique ways of struggling with issues. Everyone is creative, but creativity comes in different shapes and sizes. So the group may face conflict and disagreement. How can you most effectively deal with group problems?

▶ Prepare for potential problems. Great small groups don't just happen. Leaders help their groups maintain their identity by clearly articulating the group's purpose and by helping members of the group to stay focused on the topic. Leaders also create an atmosphere in which questions are honored and learning is valued.

▶ Practice the attitudes and skills that you want the group to learn. Small groups don't just discuss information. The group leader teaches by example the attitudes and skills needed for small group interaction: tolerance, patience, caring, and support.

▶ Remember that conflict is inevitable. Becoming a mature group is impossible without conflict. The participants in a YouthSearch group care about the topic and will express strong feelings and opinions. As the leader of the group, you can help participants identify the sources of conflict and facilitate further discussion. You may also suggest that the group members agree to disagree. Remind the youth that being members of a group means supporting and respecting one another even when they disagree.

▶ Remember that problems may be the result of diversity in the group and the growing pains of adolescence. Be sure to listen to everyone's opinion, to recognize differences, and to accept each person as a unique individual. Consider: The problem may not be the more obvious sources of conflict, but the relationships among the group members. In the disciples' relationship with Jesus, they became servants of God in their daily ministry of compassion. The relationships among the people in your YouthSearch group should help them to grow in faith and service.

Our YouthSearch Group

Name	Address	Phone Number